"GREAT SUCCESS!

Contents:

Chapter one.

Chapter Two.

Chapter Three.

About the Author:

Shalom has brought joy and peace into many lives in his generation. He is trained as a Real Estate consultant.

He studied SOP Theology with MFM. Business studies with Rufus Giwa polytechnic Owo, Graphic design and multimedia with Edusa SA and currently studying BA Multimedia in

Digital Visual Art with university of South Africa UNISA. And a Psychologist by career, also he is Associate Pastor at Entheos Family Church situated at Rooihuiskraal Centurion.
He is a partner with Kenneth Copeland Ministries. He is the CEO of Adebisi Shalom Trading Enterprises [ASTE SA] and the director of Adebisi Shalom Leadership Institute [ASLI SA] which is based in Rooihuiskraal Centurion South Africa.
His vision is to enable any man from any race to become who God has destined them to be.

Dedication: I dedicate this book! Great Success to God Almighty. I gave Him the glory for making it possible for this dream to become a reality.

ISBN Number: 978-198-323-570-2

Introduction: Great Success. Is based in prophetic, inspirational, faith building and spiritual growth! Which can be used, as a daily devotional and prayer into the will of God for one purpose in life.

Also, three chapters carefully look into:

- Dominion
- Fruitfulness and greatness
- Great Success

Dominion: as a chapter in Great Success! Some elements were carefully look into; matrix, the blessings of the womb, God grace, Achievers, By his grace, the mind set and your thought, the

seed, living in the atmosphere of dominion.

And the case study? Is the life of **Esau**. What took place when he had an encounter with his father, regard to the prophecy that was giving him! That when he have the dominion? That the yoke of his limitation will be breaking off him.

Also, the process that he took in order for his dominion to be materialize.

In other words, due to the prophecy that was giving him and the process that he took? After he left his father presences? He did overcome all the challenges that he has been experiencing with.

Also, both him and Jacob his brother that course his limitation in the first place! Were able to meet and the issues between them was solved.

In other words, **Great success**! Is also based in spiritual growth, prophetic, inspirational and faith building. Nehemiah is the case study. His life in the land of Shushan, and how he met his brethren regards to the falling walls of Jerusalem, and how he waited on God, regards to the steps to take for the rebuilding of the falling walls of Jerusalem.

Also, how he was favoured by the king and with the provision that was giving him by the king. Other mechanisms were also look into that will enable any one, which may be in needs to achieved great success in his or her life.

Fruitfulness and Greatness.

fruitfulness and greatness is also based in inspirational that will enables any one in living a fruitful life and living great at every endeavours of life.

"GREAT SUCCESS.

"**Matrix**. Having a **career in multimedia,** am taught about design and shape of an object.

Matrix? Meaning! An environment in which something develops, a mould in which something is shaped. Did we know that the destiny of Esau received a turn around, after he has had an encounter with his father? **(Genesis 27:40b NKJV)** In the same environment that his destiny was affected negatively. Genesis 22:1-29.

The environment we live in, has lot of impact to do with our lives, likewise, some environment are endowed with what i called heavenly resources on earth, in the case of Ruth in the land of Bethlehem-judah where she was favored.

Ruth chapter 2. Whereas some environment are negative, **"but"** with the help of God, negative environment can be turn to positive environment. In other word, anywhere or an environment that one was opportune to be, either through self-discovery or divine provision, there is always an opportunity in disguise, all what we need to do, is to ask God to open our eye, to see the positive reality that is around us.

Also an environment is a place of one's birth where one grows up from, before getting to an adulthood age. But unknowing to Esau that his environment will be quell at him at some certain stage of his life, an environment that he hunter and loved. (Genesis 25:27 NKJV).

I do not know where your predicament started from? May be in a particular environment. The horn of dominion is liberating you now, in Jesus name. The journey of revolution began in the Life of Esau when he has the full understanding of the fundamentals principles of an achievers that is not too late to take a move in a suffocating situation and challenge his present state with the horn of dominion.

Be known to him (Esau) that
there will be a reversal of an
event in the future. (Genesis
33:8-9 NKJV). I decree into
your Life that greatness
awaits you in the future in
Jesus name. Amen.

'' *The* blessing of the *Womb*.

**To be a blessing to your
world**, your background those
not matter, where you came
from those not matter, the
color of your skin or your
hair type has nothing to do
with the vision God has giving
you!

(**Jeremiah 1:5 NKJV**). It say's;
before I formed thee in the
belly I knew thee, and before
thou camest forth out of the
womb I sanctified thee, and I

ordained thee a prophet unto
the nation.

"So many has been asking with
in themselves, among friend,
family or in the community
that they came out from. **"WHY
ME"**! As a result of the
challenges that they are
facing with or what they are
experiencing.

And it has been resulting in
living in low esteem of life,
which is not the mandate of
God for any of his children,
to live below an achiever, or
dominion.

Your destiny is what God has
ordained, before you were form
in the womb, not after you
were giving birth to! You are,
but an original creature of
God, assigned to live in
dominion and to fulfill
destiny.

I decree, may the blessing of the womb, be upon you! Today and beyond in the name of Jesus.

I don't know? What has been the delay to your breakthrough and deliverance? It has been appointed for a woman to deliver on the ninth month.

I pray in this season of the year, you will fulfill in the name of Jesus. And favor, goodness, breakthrough, deliverance will be your portion IJN.

In other words, your present state does not determine your future! Your life is in God hands, and he will guide and leads you to your blessings.

"Also when Esau came in terms with the news of what his brother has done to him, he felt all hope is gone. **(Genesis 27:32-34 NKJV).** But

he that sits in heaven says!
No your life is in my hands.

And God almighty brings is
covenants to pass in the life
of Esau for greatness.

You are nothing, but great in
the sight of God. I pray.
Dominion is your today and
beyond. Amen.

"God Grace".

**After Isaac have declare the
dominion into the life of his
son (Esau),** he went out from
his father presence, and went
about his daily lives as
hunter, not that he was
perfect in what he was doing
or either was he the best
hunter in his time.

But! Did we know there are
many hunters in his days? Some
hunter like him may even be

finding it so difficult in getting breakthrough in their hunting business, but for Esau God grace is more than enough.

Some time in his life, he may even be finding it so difficult in going out for hunting, but the grace of God in form of dominion will say to him go and possess.

Even in summer and winter when the weather is so harsh, the grace of God will come to him as dove, go! Greatness is yours.

(Song of Solomon 2:14 NKJV). O my dove, that are in the clefts of the rock, in the secret place of the stairs, let me see thy countenance, let me hear thy voice, for sweet is thy voice, and thy countenance is comely.

"Also talking about God grace! God grace can be refer to, has dominion in human lives. I decree into your life, in this month and beyond you will achieve your goals in life and you will end well in the name of Jesus. **"God grace".** (**Genesis 1:26).** And God said, let us make man in our image after our likeness, and let them have dominion over the fish of the sea, and over the fowl of the air, and over the cattle, and over all the earth, and over every creeping thing that creepeth upon the earth. Vs27. So God created man in his own image, in the image of God created he him; male and female created he them.

"In the part A of **Genesis 1:26.** It say's after our likeness. **Meaning?** it take God likeness towards mankind, in order for us, as being to take charge over what God has created for us to enjoy in life.

But many are far from these Biblical realities, in terms of taking charge and having dominion.

I decree, it will not take longer time again, this year is your year of dominion Jesus name.

"Achiever's".

Achievement is one of, great voluminous in the millennium century, and it has been a great measure that defines great achievers in our present world.

Has anyone, ever think or thought? How important is to be a great achievers in this present days, and to be an influential personality in the atmosphere of great achievers?

"All these information was discover by Esau, and he was well informed about the entire important tool, that needed to be an achievers.

Not that he was well educated or either was he well learned, but there is something in him that is so unique, that is beyond human knowledge and wisdom, which cannot be in the same equal with human ability.

Which is known as the **"spirit of dominion".** Job (32:8-9 NKJV). But there is a spirit in man, and the inspiration of the Almighty giveth them understanding. Vs9. Great men are not always wise: neither do the aged understand judgment.

"As a hunter",

Only little does he know! Not to be available in the area of his specialty, because he has spent his whole life in learning a particular skill. Which is? Hunter! And he was good at what he has acquired.

"In this text? Yours enemies might have stolen your belongings and valuable things, but they can't steal your dream.

I prophecies by the spirit of dominion, whatever you might have lost; you will recover all and overtake in the name of Jesus.

"Esau continued with his skill,

He did not dwell with the pass event, either did he think a bit about what has happened to him in the pass, because his skill is more important and precious to him, than the horrible event that he has experiences in the pass.

Also is the same skill that he was involved doing that he experiences the strange event of his Life. In other words, is in the same skill that he was involved doing that God granted him **"the dominion"** which leads to multiplication.

(**Genesis 33:8-9 NKJV**). And he said, what meanest thou by all this drove which I met? And he said. These are to find grace in the sight of my Lord vs9. And Esau said. I have enough, my brother, keep that thou hast unto thyself.

"God is looking for way to blessed you and multiply your

resources! If only you can continued and focus with your dream and skill.

Whatever might has happened that makes you to lost trust in men. Put it aside and allow God to do his work in your Life.

I pray, dominion is yours in this year and beyond in Jesus name. Amen.

"*By* his grace".

We are an achiever, not that we are qualified in the first place or skillful.

But it's by his grace we are reckoned with in the atmosphere of great achievers. **(Ephesians 2:8-9 NKJV).** For by grace are ye saved through faith, and that not of yourselves; it is the gift of

God: **vs9**. Not of work; it is the gift of God.

The grace of God in the lives of men is more than what we can fathom or imagine, he keeps and watch over us in times of horrible challenges and helping us to achieve unachievable goals and dreams! He fought our battle and making us to live in victories.

If is not by his grace, what could have been said about us or our love one's? In times of that difficulty, trials and goals that seems like mountain to climb! His grace enables us to stand out in the mix of all odds and challenges.

Today we can look back at the beginning of the year, and say! Lord it's by your grace. In other words, the grace we are thanking God for today, or in the dispensation of ours, can also be refer to the life of Esau! When everything's seems to him as a mountain to climb! In the first place.

(Genesis 27:31 – 40 NKJV). Be known to him that, he will look back after the end of the tunnel, and say! I have more than enough.

(Genesis 33:9 NKJV). Beloved, it's not every one that has the privilege to thank God? But I and you do! That is why, i know in the remaining days, week to end this year, the living lord will fill your mouth with a shout of testimony in the name of Jesus.
To those that know the beginning of Esau may think, he can never amount to any good things in life. I don't know how your beginnings were? But one thing I know, you are coming out and favor,

greatness will be your portion IJN, Amen

'' *The mind set and your thought.*

with the mind battle are won also with the mind battle are lost, the mind is a powerful weapon that determine the journey of a man on how long or how far the journey will be at the end of the day.

In the dictionary point view! The mind is the ability to be aware of things. Think and reason. The intellect. Thought; Some time ago in power of success. I text about thought, as, the happiness of our lives depends on the quality of our thought. Think good and think big.

In the dictionary point view, it says! Think, and ideal, the process of thinking attention, considerations. That is to say, the mind set and the thought are very important in the life of any one that will bless his or her world, and having dominion.

"How is the state of your mind set and your thought?

Are you at the point of giving up! On the vision, promises, sweet dream and having dominion that God has giving you? (**Number 13:1-2 NKJV**).

And the lord spoke unto Moses, saying. **vs2.** Send thou men, that they may search the land of Canaan which i give unto the children of Israel; of every tribe of their fathers shall ye send a man, everyone a ruler among them. **Vs. 18.** And see the land what it is; and the people that dwelleth there in, whether they be strong or weak few or many.

Truly speaking the land was challenging, the people there were stronger and mightier than them. **vs30.** And Caleb stilled the people before Moses, and said, Let us go up at once, and overcome it, but the other group said! **Vs31.** But the men that went up with him said, we be not able to go up against the people; for they are stronger than we.

My question is?

What group are you, are you in the group of Caleb and Joshua, that worked on their mindset and their thought, saying they will go and take the land, which the lord their God has giving them, despite how challenging it was, or are you in the other group?

The Holy Spirit said, someone is here! As you are reading this text, you are about to give up on your business and the dream God has giving you? Saying there is global crash and things are hard, He says! Be like Caleb and Joshua that worked on their mindset and their thought.

He says, he will give you good news, the end has not yet come, and this is the beginning.

Also Esau worked on his mindsets and his thought, which was recorded to him for greatness. **(Genesis 27:41 NKJV), (Genesis 33:8-9 NKJV).**

" *T*he seed.

A man of God in the 1904s by name G. Campbell Morgan says; the real future is the past, and the past is the future?

Meaning: **"by me"** your past determine your future. And am saying, now!! Is the future. Known matter what went wrong or happens in the past? You can still improve your presence.

After the seed of dominion has been sown into the life of Esau by his father in (Genesis 27:40b), and it shall come to pass when thou shalt have the dominion, that thou shalt break his yoke from off they neck.

And **(He)** Esau went out of his father presence as a change man, determined to approach is future with all strength and with the "awareness show-case to him in form of seed" that? When thou shalt have the dominion these entire strange occurrence will be no more.

I speak to your life by the awareness of the seed of dominion, all this strange circumstance in your life, will be no more in Jesus name.

Also seed sown in the past has been the result of the present. That means! Nothing will be or hold in the future when adequate of planning are not in place in our present or

in the endeavors' of our
lives.

Esau went on the atmosphere of
the awareness that he can make
a change in what look
unachievable for him and God
crown his effort with
greatness **(Deuteronomy 2:1-7
NKJV)** I see you making it in
this year and beyond.

'' *Living* in the atmosphere of dominion.

Involved with God and men!

Because it's the free gift and
commandment of God to mankind.
Has it been stated in (**Genesis
1:28 NKJV**). I don't know what
has been your challenges in

the previous year? But the living Lord is commanding you to lives in dominion in this year and beyond.

I prophesied in this year and beyond! You will be fruitful, multiply and replenish the earth in the name of Jesus. Also, in **(Genesis 27:40b NKJV)**. Isaac was saying to Esau? When thou shalt have ''**the dominion**'' that thou shalt break his yoke from off thy neck.

I declare in the name of Jesus! Whatever signified yoke of bondage in your life will be broken in the name of Jesus.

I speak to yoke of lack, poverty, sickness, failure and bewitchment to be broken off you. Oh and behold Esau reap the reward of his father decree in **(Genesis 33 verse 8-9 NKJV)**.

I pray by the end of this year! The living lord will fill your mouth with testimony in the name of Jesus.

Chapter two:Friutfulness and greatness

"Fruitfulness and Greatness.

(Deuteronomy 28:2 - 3 NKJV).
And all these blessing shall
come on thee, and overtake
thee, if thou shalt hearken
unto the voice of the Lord thy
God. Vs3. Blessed shalt thou
be in the city, and blessed
shalt thou be in the field.

"*As* the done, of a new
year in humans world,

which is appearance has not been known to many and what it takes to lives in fulfilment and to be an achiever's? Keeps to be a worrisome and difficulties to many.

Due to these, the anxiety and the certainty to success has led too many to the verge of failure before success. In other words, question has been raised, why human could not have a right perspective for a new year done, and to achieve all the goals that has be set towards it?

''there is known doubt about human having adequate knowledge and the abilities in setting a new year revolution, all of humanly capacity of achieving success, are all limit or limited when talking of receiving a revelation or mandate from God, regarding to a new year done or for a particular year.

Every year has its own agenda, and there is two players'! God and the enemies.

'' *God is the maker of heaven and earth, human and every things that is in existence in human world.*

In other worlds, he known the beginning and the ending, any things that will be in any year, are all knew to him.

For anyone to have a fulfilled year? Such one need to have a connection with him and his word! Which is the main guideline in having a fulfilled year.

I didn't know how your year were right now? I have a word for you! You will end well and finished strong in great success in the name of Jesus.

''*The enemies*.

Any one that lacks a connection with God, such ones will always find it difficult to be an achiever at any particular year. Reasons for, not been able to get edge of protection to fulfilments, has been breach.

It could be to living a sinful life style, or not having the knowledge of God, and that will result not to have adequate success.

I pray, you are coming out from all the mess of the enemies and from now on to the end of the year, you will celebrate great achievement in Jesus name. Amen.

(Psalm 3:4 NKJV). I cried unto the lord with my voice, and he heard me out of his holy hill.

' ' *T*ime and resource are vital key of abundant.

The proper use of time, enables one to lives in fruitfulness and greatness.

Time and resource? Are like nourishment that is earnestly needed in building a desire goals and achieving adequate success in life.

In other words, without time and resources, not available or present in goals building? Success, fruitfulness and greatness will always be a futile phenomenon.

''Time and resource in goals building.

Availability of time and resource enhance productivities that lead to fruitfulness and greatness.

Achievement towards desire goals that has been set from the beginning of the year? May not have been yielding to a favourable result, at present! But within us? We had made proper use of the resources and time, in order to be an achiever with in the year, but to our amazement things are not just going the way we had desire it to be. And every of our effort seems to be a futile phenomenon.

''It does not matter the result at present.

Having knowledge in God and what is capable of doing? Is

one of the priorities in goals achieving. Every things around us, may be like a mountain to climb? But the word of God in us? Is capable to bring every mountain to subjection.

If we are willing to turn to God, and utilizing our standing in him, and what his words says we are. By doing these every mountain will obey us, and things that seems unachievable will be achieved and fruitfulness and greatness will be our portion in Jesus name. Amen.

(Psalm 100:4 NKJV). Enter into his gates with thanking and into his courts with praise, be thankful unto him, and bless his name.

A heart of appreciation.

Are vital key in living in abundant and receiving endless blessings from the throne of God.

Looking back, to the beginning of the year? Where we set our utmost needs and goals for the year! At the altar of prayer.

From then to now? Lots of numerous things has happened, which some events that supposed to have! Taking our lives, could not result of us; been at the receiving end! Could be link to how merciful and loving our God is.

Also, so many blessings, success and breakthrough that I and you can count from then to now? Are the doing and grace of God! Not of our doing, either was it our abilities to achieve success. But are the mercies of God to us in achieving in life.

''Having a heart of appreciation at all time.

It does not mean? When we achieved or achievement knocking at the door of our lives, that we should appreciate God, for his goodness, protection and loving kindness in our lives.

Showing appreciation to God or having a heart of appreciation? Are continuous things that every believers in Christ have to be observing! And in so doing, many victories will be won, and many achievements will be achieved.

''All I need, is you lord.

More of God in our lives is enough to carry us through in

our journey in the year, with in the year and beyond.

Also, helping us to be an achiever. I do not know, how your year were right now? I have a word for you! You will end well in great success in Jesus name. Amen.

Psalm 150:6. Let everything that hath breath praise the Lord. Praise ye the Lord.

'' *T*he greatest success.

That anyone can count, or achievement been achieved from the beginning of the year till now? Is not only the success achieved or how blessed we are! But the greatest success is, being a living soul and living healthy in Life.

The greatest success. Are free gift from God dwelling place, which he bestow on us! That is helping us in counting our blessings, having power to make wealth and be an achieved in Life.

In other words, without being a living soul and living healthy in Life? Fruitfulness and greatness will be a forgotten journey for any one that has desired to be an achiever in Life. But thanks been to God for the gift of Life, and living healthy that he has bestowed on us.

''Having a heart of appreciation to God.

No matter, the level of our achievement, what we have achieved or what we are unable to achieved yet? We should still shows a heart of appreciation to God at all time.

Praising God and thanking him for his goodness in our lives, open doors to much more success and achievement, which unachievable by us, and helping us to fulfilled divine destiny in Life.

''Giving him the praise that is due to him.

Praises are weapon of liberation from the obstacles of the enemies, and it has been a highly weapon of deliverance in the spiritual warfare.

I pray the living Lord will fill your mouth with his praises this season and beyond! And fruitfulness and greatness will be our portion in Jesus name. Amen.

''reat, success.

(Nehemiah 1 vs 1 NKJV). The words of Nehemiah the son of Hachaliah, And it came to pass in the month Chisleu, in the twentieth year, as I was in shushan the place.

''*Your location is vitally important and where you stand*

in faith, in God are also much more important.

So many that could not achieve adequate success in the past year, and that could not count any of their dreams, vision or goals! To materialize in the area of their utmost needs? Could be link to been in a wrong location, either in the area of settlement, or wrong standing in God and in faith.

In other words, location can be refers to? As a meeting place, between us and our destiny, blessings and receiving instruction from God.

Also, being in a right location? Enables our dreams, vision and goals to materialize and achieving adequate result. Also, location can be? Who is with us, in that meeting place! And the state of our standing in faith and in God.

I pray, in this year! Wrong location, company of people and wrong standing in faith and in God, out of your life in Jesus name.

''*Your location is vitally important.*

Nehemiah, could not have achieved his purpose in life? If he was wrongly position, both in his life, the area of his settlement and in his standing in faith and in God.

To be rightly position? Enables destiny to materialize! And vision, goals and dreams achieving great success. Also, rightful connection surrounding one purpose in life.

'' Be rightly position.

For any one, to be an achiever, and to lives successful in this year? Location and been rightly position are earnestly important in the life of an individual, couples or family that desired to achieved great success in this year and beyond.

Prayer: you will be rightly position and your location, either in right standing in faith, in God or settlement will be favour by God, in Jesus name. Amen.

(Nehemiah 1:2 NKJV). That Hanani, one of my brethren, came, he and certain men of Judah, and i asked them concerning the Jews that had escaped, which were left of

the captivity, and concerning Jerusalem.

''*T*he locations, where eagles can be discover? Or gathered! Have not be discover or found, as a crowded place.

But they are gathered in a pleasant settlement! The mountain top.

The eagles are species, which are not too common to other species, which can be discovered in human habitat.

In other words, due to the uniqueness of the nature of an eagle, it makes it more

superior than any other bird!
In strength, visualizing and
achieving aim. Also, as other
species of bird gathered,
likewise! The eagles also
gathered.

''The gathering of an eagles.

Gathering of an eagles, are
not too common! To the
gathering of other species of
birds, which can be notice or
find at any giving place.
Meanwhile, when eagles
gathered! They strengthens
their self, review their
vision and sharing important
information, in order for
achieving adequate result or
success. In other words, the
location of their meeting
place? Are decently
meaningful. Such as, the
mountain top, trees and neat
sea shore.

''*Where are you Standing*.

Nehemiah could have missed his destiny! If, he was wrongly position, or standing stagnantly. Being rightly position, enables Nehemiah and other Jews family of his that are rightly minded, to connect, share and review their ambition regarding to the falling wall of Jerusalem.

In other words, nothing could have happened! If, they are in different geographical location or wrong place of destiny, or having different purpose.

Prayer: you will be rightly position in God. And where you gathered will be meaningful and favoured by God. In Jesus name. Amen.

53

(Nehemiah 1:3 NKJV). And they said unto me. The remnant that are left of the captivity there in the provinces are in great affliction and reproach, the wall of Jerusalem also is broken down, and the gate there of are burned with fire.

''Great vision and goals, are what that has been impacted and seasoned by God with grace and favour, in affecting Humans world positively, turning soul to

rightly positions in God!

And helping them in having ease access to their divine purpose and destiny in life.

Every destiny or purpose of a man that has been seasoned or endowed by God for greatness and favour! Has been included in God divine frame work, in order to affect the remnants that are directly or indirectly connected to God divine frame work.

In other words, the remnant can be refers to? To those that God has included to his divine frame work or those that he attached to us, in order to affect their purpose in life, turning them to God and helping them to have an ease access to their purpose in life.

''The remnants.

A remnant or remnants are not an object! But they can be refers to, as living things, soul or a person. That lacks the cutting edge in achieving and living great in life. They may have tried their possibility? Of achieving.

Due to their humanly, or not having much knowledge about God divine frame work? Making them to think God is far away from them! The remnants. But their progress has been attached to God divine frame work.

Nehemiah? Can be refers! To as God master frame work, which God endowed and favour his dreams, vision and purpose. In order to make an impact in the may streams of God frame work! In affecting, saving and rebuilding the falling walls of Jerusalem.

In other words, every achievement or blessings that God has blessed us with? Has been designed by God to affect his frame works, not only just for us only to enjoy it.

''*God divine frameworks*.

God is a God of knowledge and his all-knowing God, and God of abundant. He lifteth up and bringeth low.

1 Samuel 2:7. The lord maketh poor, and maketh rich; he bringeth low, and lifteth up.

In other words, God frame works is what he has designed to impact the remnants that may be lacking the cutting edge of success in life.

Prayer: in this year and beyond! God will endow your vision, goals, purpose and destiny in life with great success of his and your success will affect God divine frame works in Jesus name. Amen.

(Nehemiah 1:4 NKJV). And it came to pass, when I heard these words, that I sat down and wept, and mourned certain days, and fasted, and prayed before the God of heaven.

"**S**eeds of divine leaders are mountain movers! Just has destiny are made, make and shape.

Also, a leader is made, make and shape. Seeds of divine leaders are not too common as other species of bird that can be found or notices at any giving place. They are, as an eagle that can be discovered or gathered in a pleasant settlement, the mountain top. Also, they are decently endowed with great vision and goals by God to fulfilled in life.

In other words, they were not move by the challenges or pressures that may be confronting them, or their vision or goals in life! At times, they may be emotional? Because they are humans.

Been human or humanly, does not mean! That, they are succumbed to the challenges facing them in life. But they have a God who strengthens and empowering them to achieved great success and goals in life.

"Been human or humanly does not mean succumbed to the challenges of life.

All what God want from his seeds? Is, to find a seating position! Any time that challenges are confronting them in life.

A seating position? A seating position can be identified as a resting place, refreshing, energizing and a place of empowerment! Where God identified for all his seeds that may needs his divine intervention at any stages of their lives.

"A seating position.

Nehemiah identified or concluded that his present

situation or challenges can never be solve or achieved by his strength! Rather finding a resting place in the God of all things. By him, identified his seating position in God Almighty? That enables him to achieve the great success and impacted life.

Prayer: at any challenges that may be confronting you in life! May you identify your seating position in God. And great success will be achieved by you! In Jesus name. Amen.

(Nehemiah 1:10 NKJV). Now these are thy servants and thy people, whom thou hast redeemed by thy great power, and by thy strong hand.

"*T*he joy that beyond all riches and abundant, is not in what we have or what we are able to acquired or achieved.

But unending and lasting joy we may desired to have in life? Is the joy of salvation.

Our salvation or the joy of salvation that we have! Is, what that covenant every believers in Christ into the abundant blessings and favour of God.

We have been saved not of corruptible seed, but of

incorruptible seed! In showing forth the beauty of the living lord, and we are the redeemed of the lord God. In other words, in the journey of faith and believes in God, at time? It may be dusty and narrow! How dusty and narrow it is? Does not determined, we have been forgotten or neglected by God.

But in the dusty and narrow experience of our journey in life? If, only! We can call on the name of the living lord, and to seek his face in prayers, every of our blessings we work accordingly, to how it has been plan by God.

"We are the redeemed of the lord.

The Jews family or the Israeli are experiencing the dusty and narrow experience of their walk and Christian faith in God.

But looking closing deeply into their genealogy from Abraham down to Jacob? They have been covenanted and redeemed by God for greatness and abundant in life, just as every one of us, the believers! But at a point or in the cause of their journey? They are experiencing unusual circumstances or strange event! Just as any one of us, that believes in Christ Jesus.

Also, the strange dusty and narrow experience that question their covenant and their promises in God! Could not face the test of time, when Nehemiah remembers God of their covenant with him. In other words, God is not a forgotten God! Is, looking for a Nehemiah! That will seek his face, and called upon his Holy Name.

Beloved! If, only we can be like Nehemiah? Our dusty and narrow experiences will be our stepping stone to our greatness and abundant in life.

"Our God is not a forgotten God.

The Jews family or the Israeli, in the time of their challenges? They did not succumb to it! They still carried the covenant of God and his promises for their life.

Even to our surprise! Did we known? That, their challenges and circumstances, knew that they are! The carrier of God promises?

I have a word for you today. In your dusty and narrow challenges, you are coming out and victory will be yours in

Jesus name. You are the redeemed of the living lord.

Prayer: the strength of Nehemiah will be seen in you. And you will be great in life in Jesus name. Amen.

(Nehemiah 2:2 NKJV). Wherefore the king said unto me, why is thy countenance sad, seeing thou art not sick? This is nothing else but sorrow of heart. Then i was very sore afraid.

''*It does not matter, our geographical locations, our*

physical position or standing, when communicating with the living Lord.

The living lord is omnipresence and omniscience, his presences his see and hear all our heart cry! Anytime we went to his presences for every of our needs, concern and fellowshipping with him, at any time or space of time, that we communicate with him? There is always a tremendous reply or feedback from his dwelling place, which he reply to all our request, prayers that we altar at his presences.

At time? He may reply to us immediately while still communicating with him in his presences or manifest his greatness in our lives in a mysteries that beyond our fathom of understanding.

Also, at any time we went to his presences for every of our concern or needs? He has never turn any one down! He always replied. **In his nature**? His ever present in attending to us and hearing our heart cry.

''*Omnipresence and omniscience*.

God is ever present and he sees to every hidden thing in our lives, before we went to him? He knows everything in our lives and he has the lasting, healthy living and solutions are all with him.

Also, the beginning and the conclusion to solving, every of our worrisome circumstances and challenges is with him, he is the God of our solution.

''The God of solution.

It beyond human intelligences and reasons, at time! When God decide to manifest his greatness or brings solution to some challenges situation that was altar at his presences.

For Nehemiah to be asked by the king regard to his difficulties which he was experiences at that point in time and how he was sad in the king presences? In the history of a cupbearer, that serves a king? It has not been recorded or finds any that was sad in the presences of a king! It will always leads to the death of such cupbearer.

In other words, it shows that the living Lord, can use any things to bring solutions to any problem or challenges that we may be facing with in Life! To show to all humans that!

All power in heaven and on earth belong to him.

Prayer: in this seasons of your life, the living Lord will show his greatness in your life and every of your heart cry to him? Will received an immediate response from his throne in Jesus name. Amen.

(Nehemiah 2:6 NKJV).Then the king said unto me, (the queen also sitting by him,) for how long shall thy journey be? So it pleases the king to send me, and i set him a time.

'' *Great* success.

Is a continuous success that lies with an individual or

collectives that desire in achieving tremendous and abundant success! With the capacity of their readiness and how well knowledge they are in approaching the dwelling place of God, which is also known as? His presences. In getting heavenly divine approaching to their divine purpose driven goals in life.

There are personal dreams, goals and vision! Also, there is vision, dreams and goals that involved collectives. The materializing or the oil of achieving lies in how readiness one is, and how knowledge one is to seek God divine intervention to the achieving process and ending.

In other words, no one is an expert in making and achieving great success in Life. There are successes! To some, or many? Success could be?

Planning to do something with in a space of time or seasons and achieving the process and the ending result. But in this prophetic Book! We are studying on! **''Great Success''**. Which involved God! That leads to continued achievement.

''Great success, lies with individuals and collectives.

Getting a big break in life, is more than just planning and setting a vision. But, achieving a big break in one desirable goal involved in, how? Diligences, discipline, hardworking and with the knowledge that one has, about God.

God! Is, the only, the right source of every vision and dreams that beyond, the intelligent of one is, in

Life. And great success is beyond human intelligences and capacity.

''Great success, is beyond humans intelligences and capacity.

It could have been a wrong statement, that! After, Nehemiah met his brethren regard to the falling walls of Jerusalem? That he went to build it, with his own capacity and intelligences.

But, the rightful statement is? He waited and enquired from God! Who owns the great success. At, every waiting and enquiring from the dwelling place of God? There is, always! A feedback, regard to the materializing achieving process. He was send, guided and was protected through the starting to the finishing.

Prayer: I pray in the hand of God! For protecting and guide through the very start of your vision, goals and dreams into your life. To the finishing ending. In Jesus name. Amen.

(Nehemiah 2:9 NKJV). Then i went to the governors in the region beyond the river, and gave them the king's letter. Now the king had sent captains of the army and horsemen with me.

'' When the hand of God, is in a man life, for success? It does

not leave the recipient of the blessings with in a perimeter of distances!

Its enables and equipped the recipient for a continued grace success. Which make or favoured the individual or collectives that are in a process of accomplishing a vision or goals.

The great success of God! That has been activated or active in a man life? Does principles that are involved in? Successful achieving and spiritual guidance.

Successful achieving:

In the principles of success?
That is involved in achieving
successful result, towards the
vision or goals that may has
been set with in a particular
timing frame! Having proper
insight and how all the
process will work in order for
a tremendous result is great
fully important in the
principles of success.

''Spiritual guidance.

Not only did the grace success
of God enable one to achieved
tremendous success, while in a
process of achieving a vision
or goals, with in a time
frame! The grace success of
God provides or enables one to
be protected in time of
spiritual or physical battles.

Talking of battles? Is a
normal phenomenon occurrences
that must humans, always
engaged with in life. But,
what that will determine? If

an individual or collectives that are engaging in a battle! Whether physical or spiritual? Is, who they lies their confident or believes in.

But, when the great success of God, is in active! In a man life? Physical or spiritual warfare will always be a stepping stone to the great success of God in the life of the recipient or collectives, that is or in the process of achieving.

''Father I need your touch.

All what any lover of God, may be desiring to emulate in life? Is the divine touch of the father into his or her life. The touch of God, in the life of Nehemiah? Distinguish him! From the process to the achieving ending.

Prayer: In this season of
your life? The divine touch of
God will see you through
from the process to the
achieving ending in Jesus
name. Amen.

(Nehemiah 2:10 NKJV). When
Sanballat the Horonite and
Tobiah the Ammonite official
heard of it, they were deeply
disturbed that a man had come
to seek the well-being of the
children of Israel.

''To
accomplished a
project, are
normal activities

and vision towards the target time and season which the visionary has projected or set in accomplishment what has been projected or set!

From the onset process toward the accomplishing ending.

But there are other elements or natural or spiritual phenomenon that must visionary of a project or those that desired in achieving their dreams! Which are not putting into consideration or paying an attention into.

The first elements are the recipes and cost that will enable one projected ambition or vision to become a reality! Such as: Location, recipient that will benefit from the project accomplished, financial and the cost of the project and timing.

''Natural phenomenon.

We may be doubting at time that natural phenomenon? Does not have any substantial effect or has any things to affect our projected dreams and vision.

But while residing outside West Africa nation! I find out that natural phenomenon has a substantial effect in one projected vision and dreams, for an instances? The weather in West Africa countries are all the same from the beginning of the year to the end of the year.

Whereas, other Southern African nations, such as South Africa, Western countries, American nations and Asia. Always has a different weather climate than any other Africa nations! In terms of; winter, spring and summer.

Anyone living in this kind of weather climates needs a proper precautions when and how to utilize, set and implements their projected dreams and vision.

''*Spiritual phenomenon.*

To Nehemiah? Spiritual phenomenon does not have any ringing in his mind! From the onset process and when provision was giving him by the king. Not of any, of spiritual confrontations was ever rings in his mind, will ever come across his vision towards rebuilding the falling wall of Jerusalem.

But in these contexts? Mentioning spiritual phenomenon could be! Unseen enemies or see enemies. But for Nehemiah he confronted with spiritual phenomenon! Which is, seen enemies that heard about his projected vision.

There are always elements either natural, spiritual phenomenon or the elements that have mentioned earlier on.

But for those that have God as their father and saviour! No need of been worried or fearful in the time of all these elements. In the cause of the remaining series? Much of insight will be carefully look into! How to challenge and overcome every elements in our projected dreams and vision.

Prayer: From your onset process of your projected goals to the ending! Divine grace success will see you through in the name of Jesus. Amen.

(Nehemiah 2:13 NKJV). And i went out by night through the valley Gate to the serpent well and the Refuse Gate, and viewed the walls of Jerusalem which were broken down and its gate which were burned with fire.

''Starting on a project, there are always time of studying the

whole meaning of the project,

the potential of the project and all that will be needed, in is accomplishment from the starting process to the finishing ending.

In any, potentials and sustainable project? Having a right perspective, from the onset process, and adequately connecting and putting in place all what that will be needed! From the onset process and to the accomplishing ending process? Are what that make a sustainable achievable result in any projected vision or goals in humans lives.

We all need, these great recipes in all our projected dreams, goals and vision that we may be desiring to achieved, or what we may have in our mind to achieve at any space of time.

In other word, Nehemiah was able to understand what he ought to do from his onset process and adequately connecting his thought and with his whole being to utilize the recipes of accomplishing his projected goal from his onset process to the accomplishing ending.

''Nehemiah recipes from his onset process.

At first, he was divinely place in a rightful location and surrounded with rightful people, environment and potential place of future resources.

When he heard about the news of the falling walls of Jerusalem? He didn't run away from what has already been built by him, or what has been divinely endowed with.

Nehemiah first recipes from his onset processes?

- He sat
- He fasted and seek the face of God
- Waited for his reply from God dwelling place
- Was able to give accurate timing
- Understood what he ought to do
- Utilizing the resources given to him
- knowing the sources of his supply

''*Your sitting and your projected goals.*

Sitting is what that ease the anxiety of any first confrontation circumstance, that relax the humans thinking of imagination of a fathoming what and what will be adequately needed for a sustainable solution.

Also, our sitting in any projected or confrontation? Are what that ease the anxiety and bringing a lasting solution. And these are one of Nehemiah recipes of accomplishment. Other recipes will be look into in the next series.

Prayer: the grace of understanding what that will be needed of you! In any projected goals or any confrontation that you may be experiencing with in life in Jesus name. Amen.

(Nehemiah 2:17 NKJV). Then i said to them, ''You see the distress that we are in, how Jerusalem lies waste, and its gates are burned with fire. Come and let us build the wall of Jerusalem, that we may no longer be a reproach.

'' *G*reat Success.

From the previous series? We have look into what enables Nehemiah to achieve his projected vision, goals and rebuilding the falling walls of Jerusalem. The first recipe that enables him was? He sat.

Our sitting in any first confrontations or

circumstances? Enables us to be ease from anxiety and having a proper direction and with the best mechanism that we may thought is best to use in any first confrontations or circumstances.

Likewise, the whole situation in our first circumstances or confrontation? Depend in our person! Who we are, what we are able to learn, our instinct, the faculty of our reasons, the location where we are, at that point in time and our believes.

All these elements were in build in the life of Nehemiah! His instinct, faculty of reasons, the location where he was, at that point in time, what he was able to learn and his believes in God. Due to all these elements used by Nehemiah? He was able to sat and utilize all the recipes that i have mentioned in the previous series.

''*The recipes that enables Nehemiah to achieved his projected vision and goals.*

He was able to fast and to seek the face of God. There is no how Great Success can be given to any one that confess to be imitator of Christ or any one that daily seeking the face of God! Either in studying the scripture or to seek the face of God for a direction in life! That would not discipline his or her body in terms of fasting and prayer.

To seek the face of God in fasting and prayer? Are divine instructions giving by the lord Jesus that we all imitate.

(**Matthew 17:21 NKJV**). Jesus was saying to his disciples? That this kind does not go out except by fasting and prayer.

Also, when one seek the face of God in fasting and prayer? Regard to one projected vision or goal in life? It provides divine intervention from the throne of God, which supply physical resources in the present process to the accomplishing ending.

''*Present process and accomplishing ending*.

The immediate of Nehemiah in his projected vision and goal in rebuilding of the falling walls of Jerusalem? Was well manage and utilize which enables supply and resources to be well available to him in his immediate Journey and having the support of willing and reputable people that join hand with him in rebuilding of

the   falling   walls   of
Jerusalem.

Your waiting in God in fasting
and prayer? Enables resources
and   supply   to   be   well
available in   your   projected
goals, vision and with the
support   of   willing   and
reputable people   in   the
journey of your projected goal
and vision.

Prayer: the grace to wait on God in fasting and prayer into your Christianity journey. Amen.

(Nehemiah 2:18 NKJV). And i told them of the hand of my God which had been good upon me, and also of the king's words that he had spoken to me, so they said, 'Let us rise

*up and build''. Then they set
their hands to this good work.*

''*Y*our waiting in God in fasting and prayer?

**Enables resources and supply
to be well available in your
projected goal,** vision and
with the support of willing
and reputable people in the
journey of your projected goal
and vision.

Waiting on God after a time of
seeking his face! Either in
praying, fasting or other miss
of waiting on God?
Distinguished an imitator of
Christ from other that didn't
imitate Christ.

Our waiting is what that gave
way to the future purpose!
Because without us waiting on

God, after seeking his face? Most of instruction will not be given and more purpose will not been achieved in the future.

As it has already be known, that the future has it effect or link with our present and our immediate! Symbolize our future.

''Blessed are those that wait on God.

To wait on God, for a particular replied after a time of seeking his face? Does not mean one is without knowledge or one his missing his or her way in life.

In other word, to wait on God? Signified how wise one is. And not every one that is waiting on God for a particular direction or what to do in life! Either in business, marriage, academic or in

ministries? Can be regards to
unwise. Meanwhile, waiting on
God? Path the way for the
future resources and achieving
success.

''*Future resources and success achieved.*

Nehemiah completes the
rebuilding of the falling
walls of Jerusalem in **Nehemiah
12.** And he celebrates it with
the Israelis. Such
accomplishments would not have
been recorded **''if''** he?
Nehemiah had not have allow
itself to utilize all the
recipes that I have mentioned.

In terms of finding a sitting
place in God, to seek God face
in fasting and prayer, waiting
for his replied from God
dwelling place, able to give
accurate timing, understanding
what he ought to do, utilizing
the resources given to him and

knowing the sources of his supply.

We all needs God, as an imitator of him in our immediate and future purpose in life and with the direction of accomplishing any projected vision or goal that we may have set in life.

Prayer: the grace to be a true imitator of Christ at every day of your life in Jesus name. Amen. God bless you.

" **G**reat success"...

BOOKS WRITTEN BY SHALOM:

Getting a Big break

Why Black Why Not White

Lord you are my deliverer

More of you lord

Living beyond the limit

Secret of an Imitator

Vision and you

You will know

Reasons

Great success

The Secret of an Achievers

Dominion: Sermon

The key of Success: Sermon

Hour of Solution with Jesus:
Sermon

BOOKS WRITTEN BY SHALOM:

Filter and taking away the chaff

Excellent God

The peculiar

The children of Zebedee

Free from the trapped

He call

Shalom is the director of; Adebisi shalom leadership institute, is a ministries which is based in Rooihuiskraal Centurion. And the C.E.O of Adebisi Shalom Trading Enterprises

South Africa.

For prayers and counseling?

Send your request to: aslileadership@gmail.com

Website site: aste-sa.business.site

Made in the USA
Middletown, DE
06 March 2020